HAL•LEONARD

GUITAR

PLAY•ALONG

Slow BLUES

Play 8 Songs with Tab and Sound-alike Audio

ISBN 978-1-4234-5345-1

HAL•LEONARD®
CORPORATION

7777 W. BLUEMOUND RD. P.O. BOX 13819 MILWAUKEE, WI 53213

Visit Hal Leonard Online at
www.halleonard.com

CONTENTS

GUITAR NOTATION LEGEND

THE MUSICAL STAFF shows pitches and rhythms and is divided by bar lines into measures. Pitches are named after the first seven letters of the alphabet.

TABLATURE graphically represents the guitar fingerboard. Each horizontal line represents a string, and each number represents a fret.

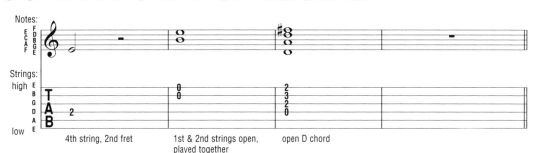

4th string, 2nd fret   1st & 2nd strings open, played together   open D chord

HALF-STEP BEND: Strike the note and bend up 1/2 step.

WHOLE-STEP BEND: Strike the note and bend up one step.

GRACE NOTE BEND: Strike the note and immediately bend up as indicated.

SLIGHT (MICROTONE) BEND: Strike the note and bend up 1/4 step.

BEND AND RELEASE: Strike the note and bend up as indicated, then release back to the original note. Only the first note is struck.

PRE-BEND: Bend the note as indicated, then strike it.

VIBRATO: The string is vibrated by rapidly bending and releasing the note with the fretting hand.

PALM MUTING: The note is partially muted by the pick hand lightly touching the string(s) just before the bridge.

HAMMER-ON: Strike the first (lower) note with one finger, then sound the higher note (on the same string) with another finger by fretting it without picking.

PULL-OFF: Place both fingers on the notes to be sounded. Strike the first note and without picking, pull the finger off to sound the second (lower) note.

LEGATO SLIDE: Strike the first note and then slide the same fret-hand finger up or down to the second note. The second note is not struck.

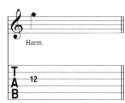

SHIFT SLIDE: Same as legato slide, except the second note is struck.

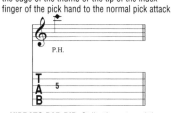

TRILL: Very rapidly alternate between the notes indicated by continuously hammering on and pulling off.

TAPPING: Hammer ("tap") the fret indicated with the pick-hand index or middle finger and pull off to the note fretted by the fret hand.

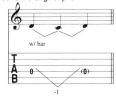

NATURAL HARMONIC: Strike the note while the fret-hand lightly touches the string directly over the fret indicated.

PINCH HARMONIC: The note is fretted normally and a harmonic is produced by adding the edge of the thumb or the tip of the index finger of the pick hand to the normal pick attack.

TREMOLO PICKING: The note is picked as rapidly and continuously as possible.

VIBRATO BAR DIVE AND RETURN: The pitch of the note or chord is dropped a specified number of steps (in rhythm), then returned to the original pitch.

VIBRATO BAR SCOOP: Depress the bar just before striking the note, then quickly release the bar.

VIBRATO BAR DIP: Strike the note and then immediately drop a specified number of steps, then release back to the original pitch.

Additional Musical Definitions

   *(accent)* • Accentuate note (play it louder).

   (staccato) • Play the note short.

D.S. al Coda • Go back to the sign (𝄋), then play until the measure marked "*To Coda*," then skip to the section labelled "**Coda.**"

D.C. al Fine • Go back to the beginning of the song and play until the measure marked "*Fine*" (end).

Fill • Label used to identify a brief melodic figure which is to be inserted into the arrangement.

N.C. • Harmony is implied.

 • Repeat measures between signs.

  • When a repeated section has different endings, play the first ending only the first time and the second ending only the second time.

Catfish Blues

Words and Music by Robert Petway

Tune down 1/2 step:
(low to high) Eb-Ab-Db-Gb-Bb-Eb

Intro
    Slow Blues ♩. = 68

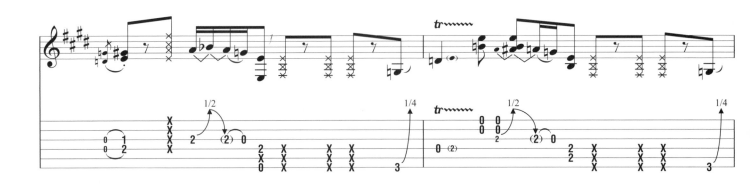

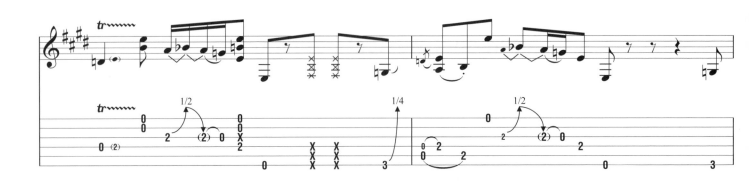

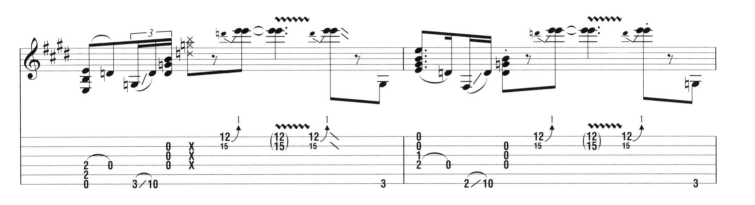

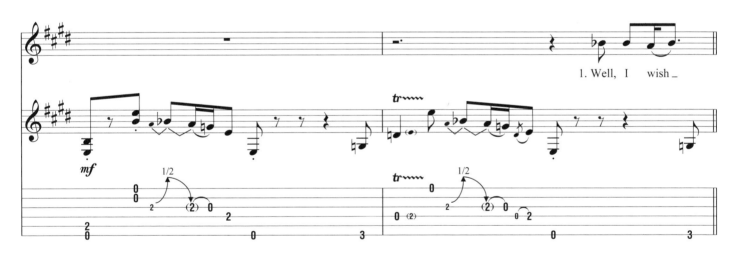

1. Well, I wish _

Verse

N.C.(E)

I _ was a cat-fish

swim-min' in, _

Oh, ___ yeah!

Oh, yeah. ___

let ring – – ┤

_mf_

fuzz dist. off

Yeah!

2. Well, now I went down

Oh, _____ yeah! _____

Oh, yeah!

w/ fuzz dist.

Oh, yeah. _____

Guitar Solo

N.C.(E7)

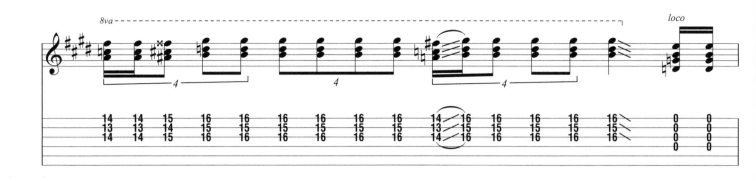

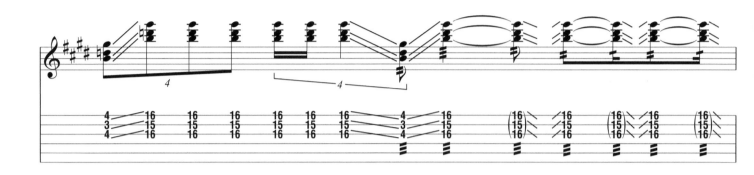

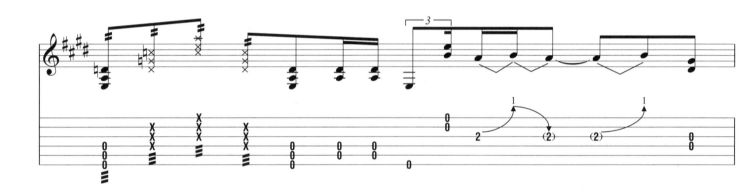

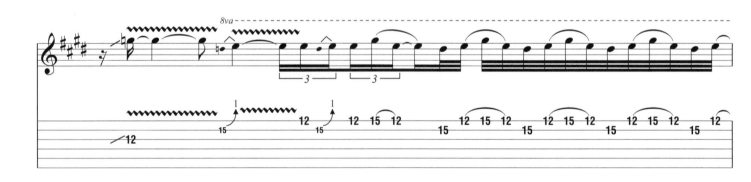

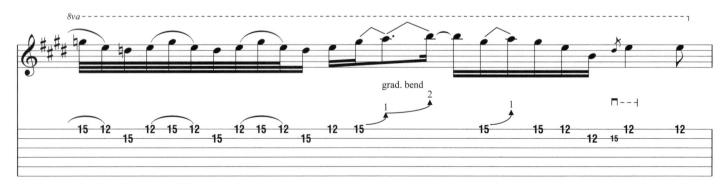

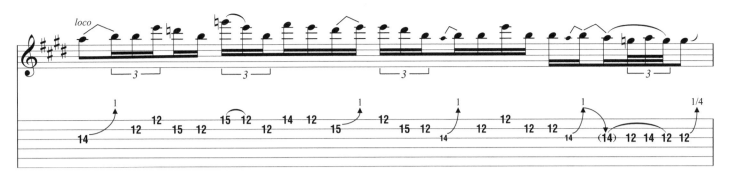

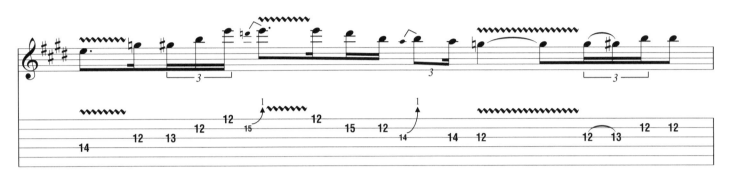

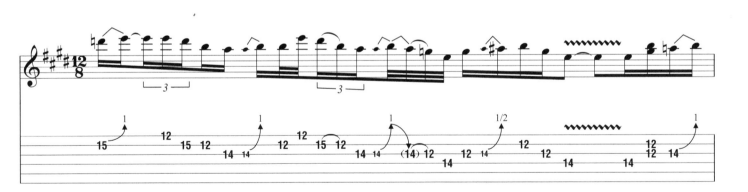

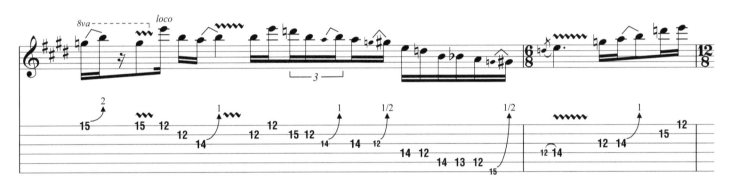

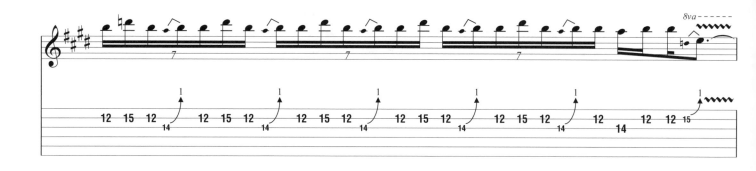

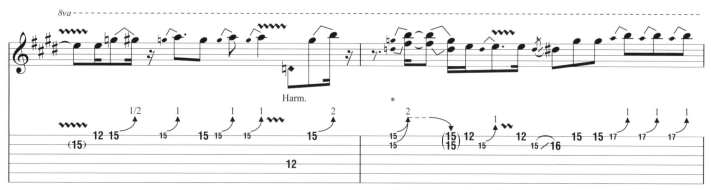

*Bend both notes w/ same finger.

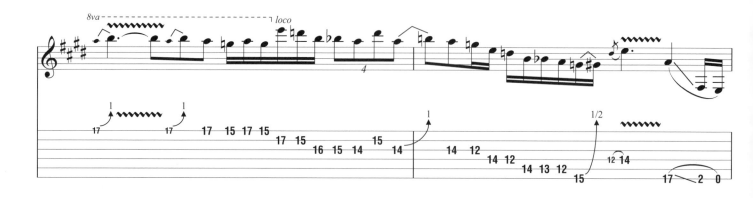

3. Well, __ there's two, __

*Vol. knob swell.

Oh, well.   Oh, yeah.

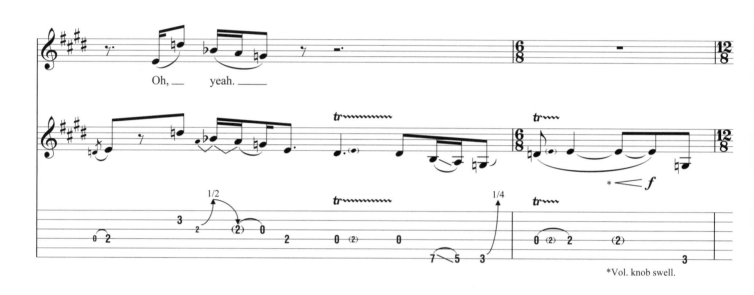

Oh, ___ yeah. ___

*Vol. knob swell.

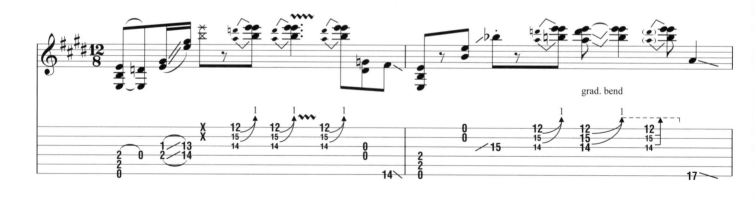

grad. bend

Drum Solo

Free time

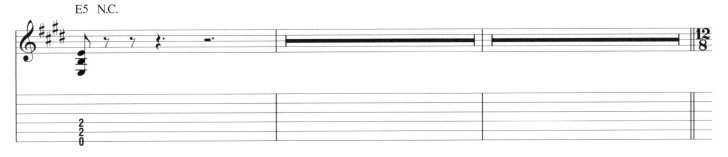

Guitar Solo
A tempo

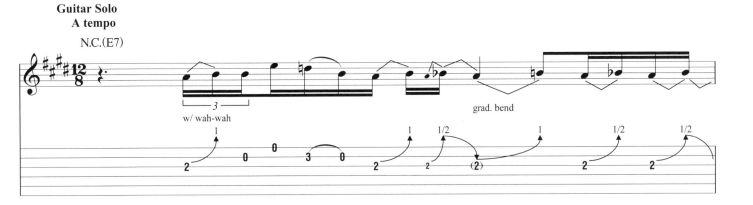

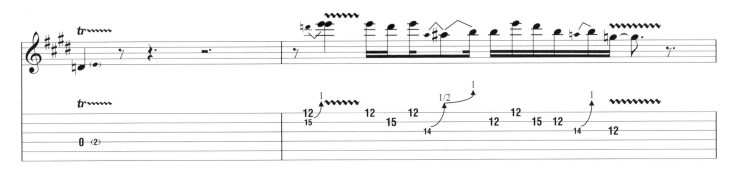

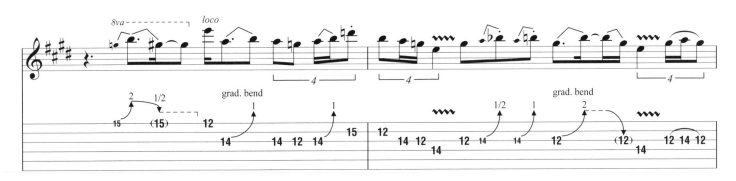

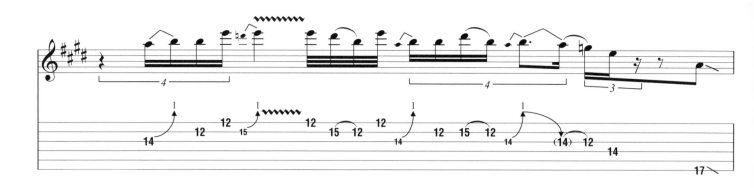

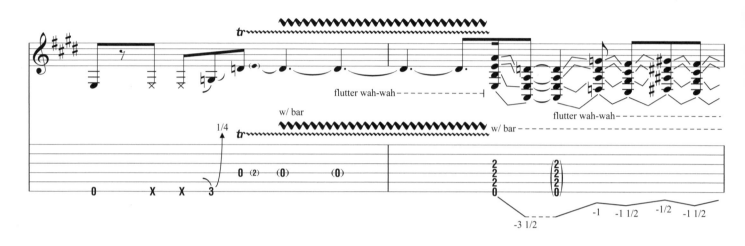

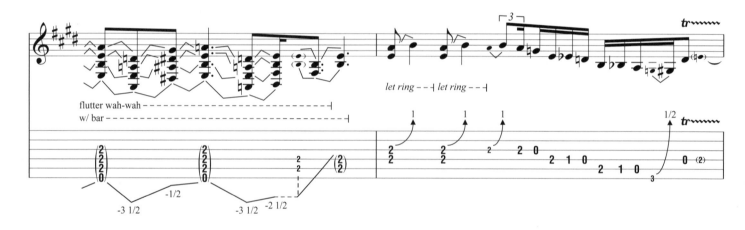

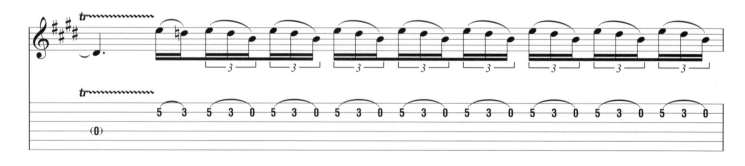

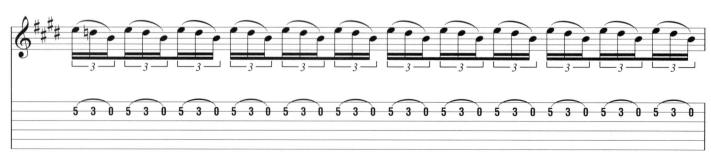

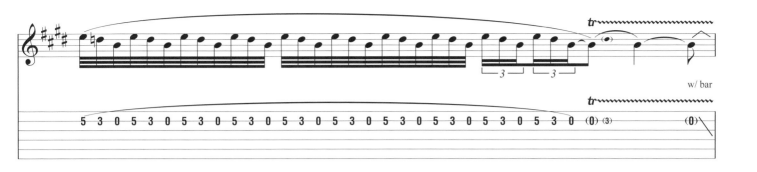

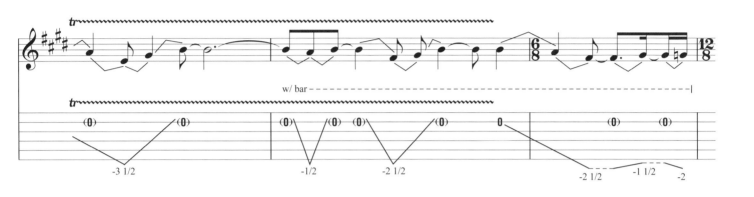

Outro-Guitar Solo

Fast Shuffle ♩ = 180 (♫ = ♪♪³)

N.C.(E7)

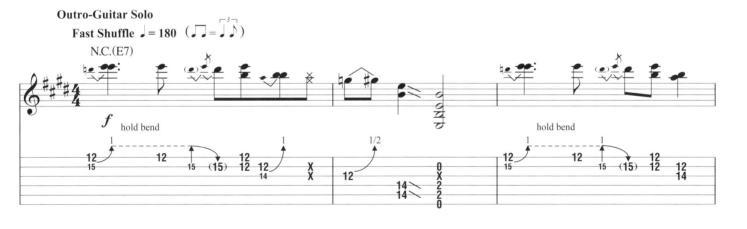

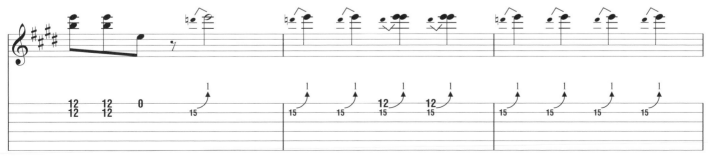

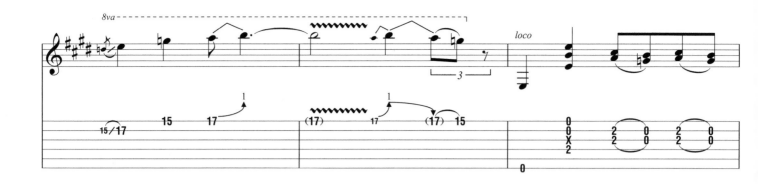

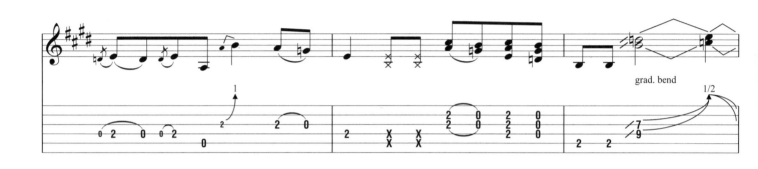

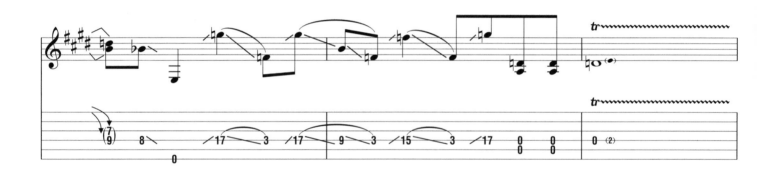

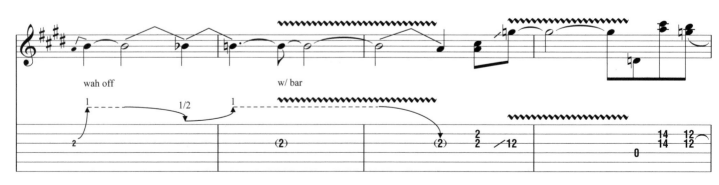

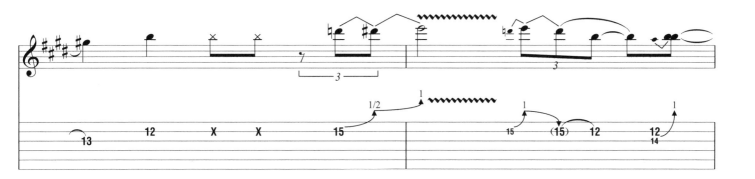

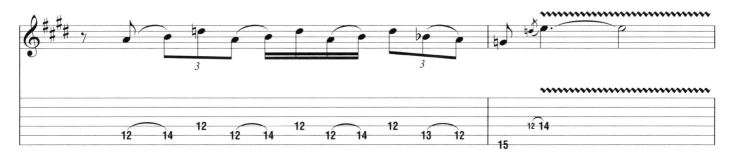

*Played as even eighth notes.

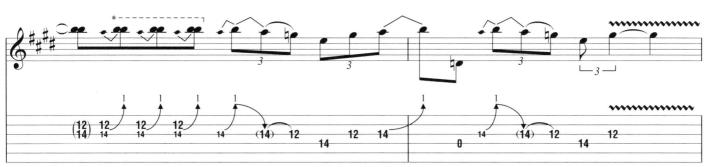

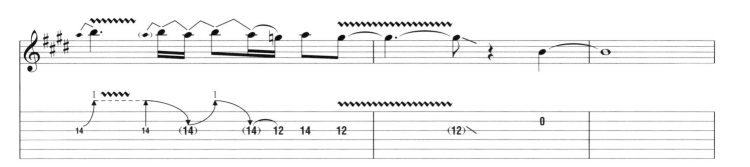

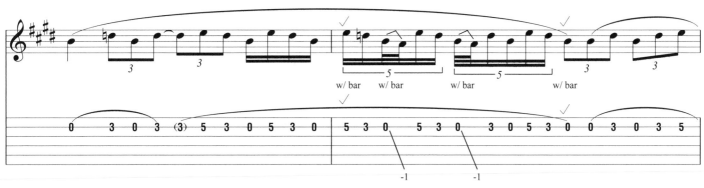

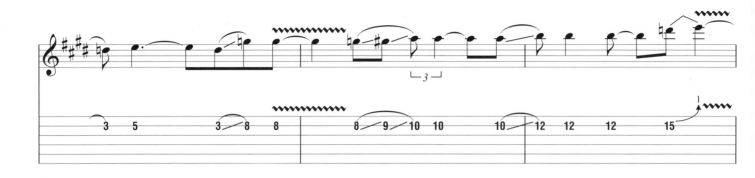

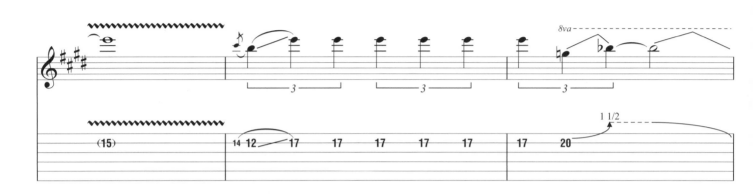

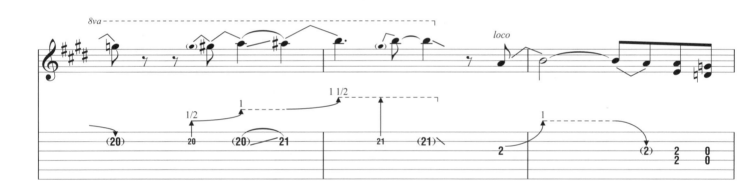

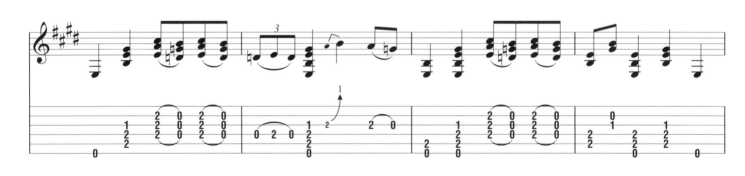

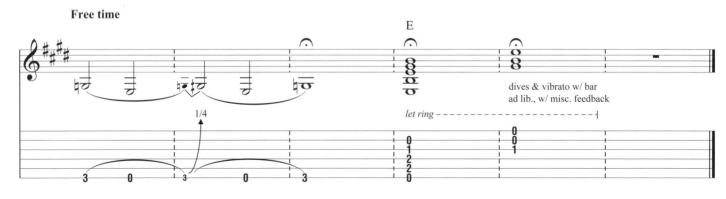

Dirty Pool

Written by Stevie Ray Vaughan and Doyle Bramhall

Tune down 1/2 step:
(low to high) Eb-Ab-Db-Gb-Bb-Eb

Intro
  Slow Blues ♩. = 52

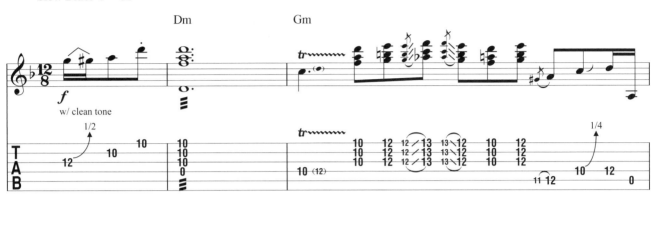

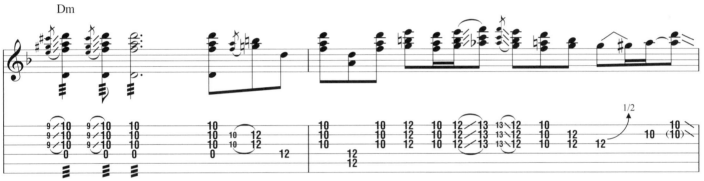

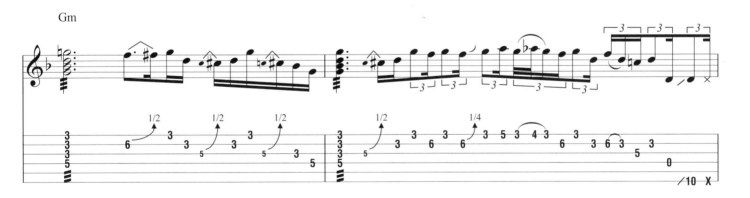

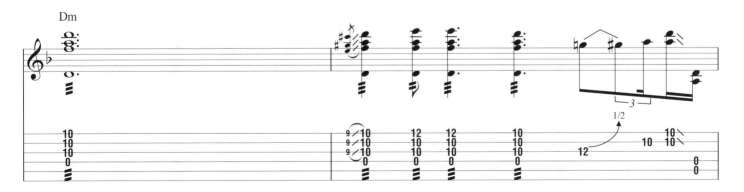

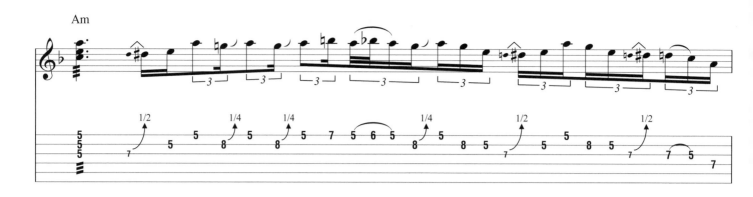

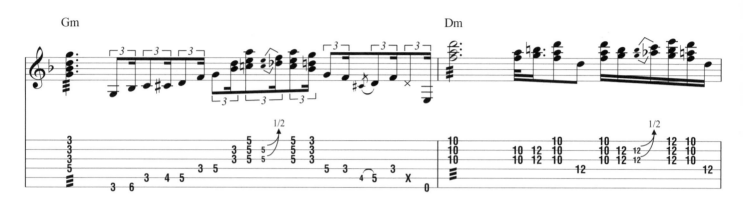

Verse

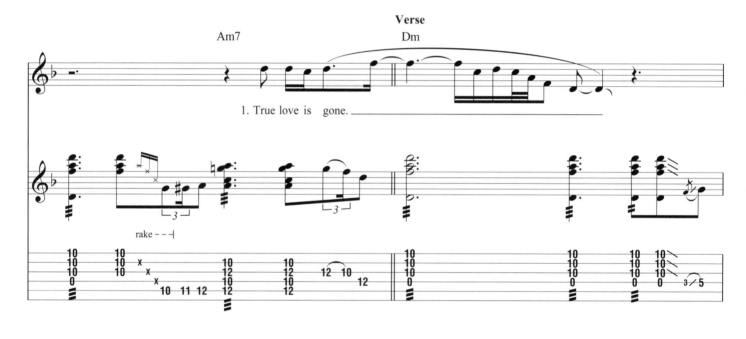

1. True love is gone. _____

I's ___ been played ___ for a fool. _____

True   love is   gone._____

*Thumb on 6th stg. throughout, where applicable.

I's___ been played___   for a   fool._____

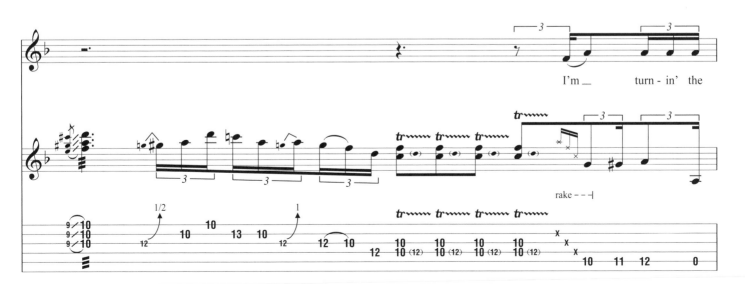

I'm ___   turn - in' the

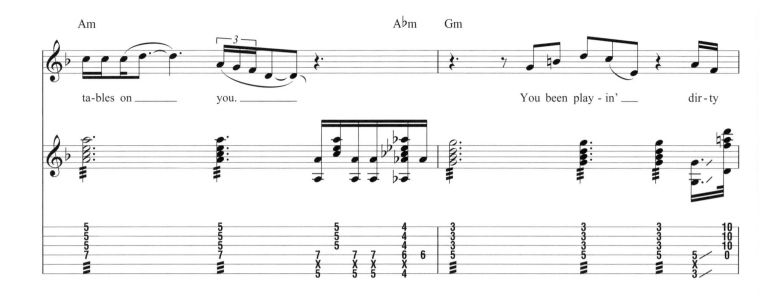

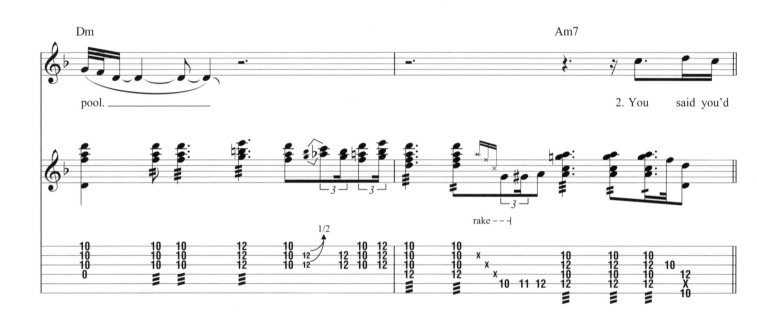

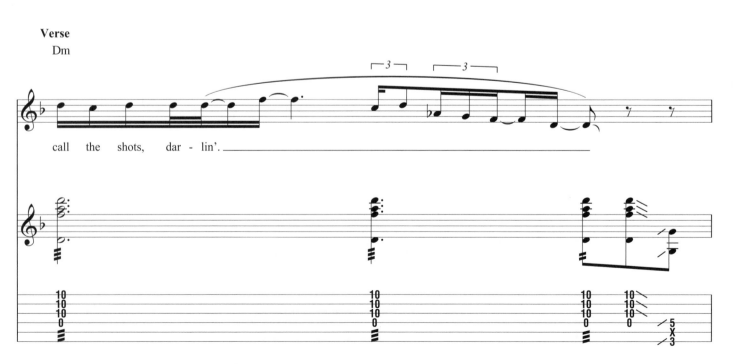

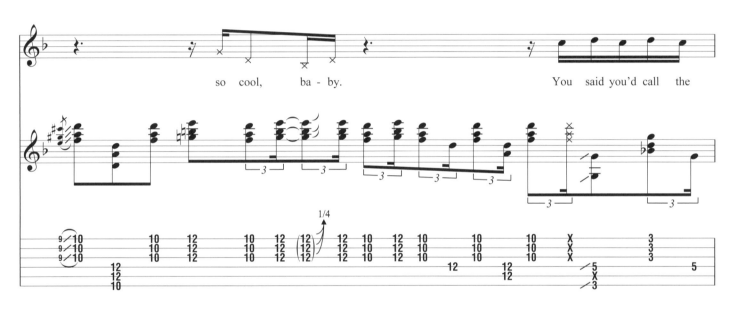

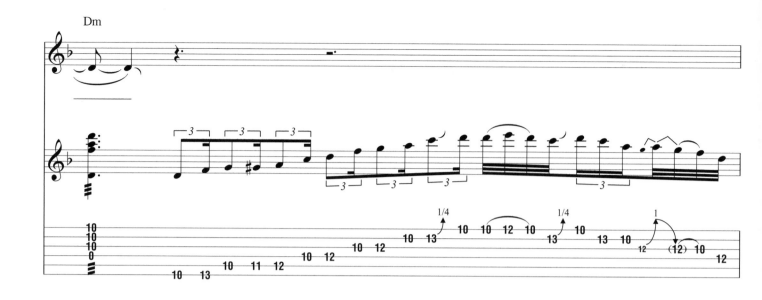

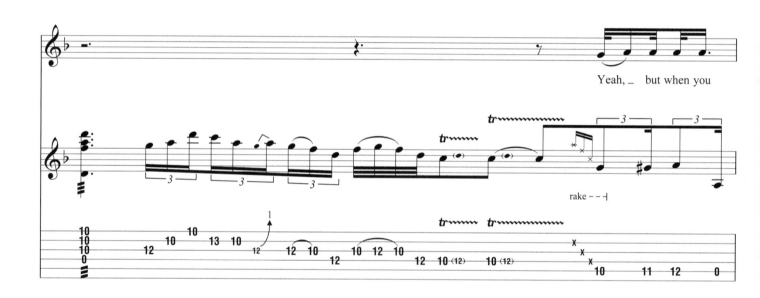

Yeah, _ but when you

shot in the eight ball, ba - by, _____

I _____ knew you were play - in' _____ 'n dirt - y

pool. _____

Guitar Solo

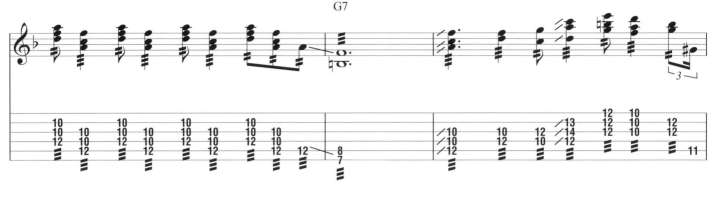

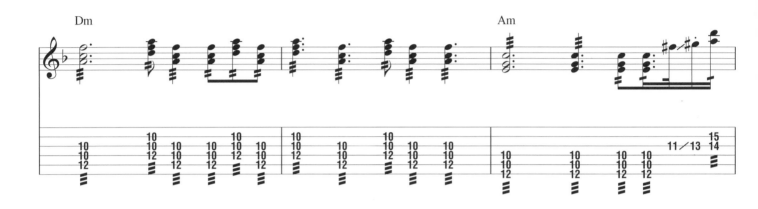

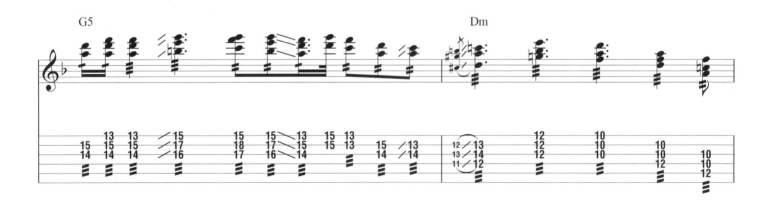

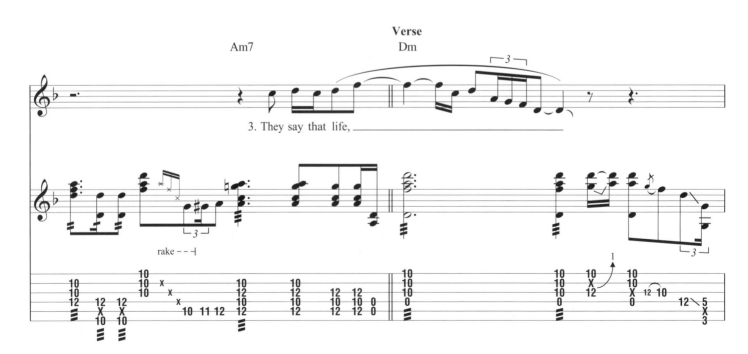

3. They say that life,

rake

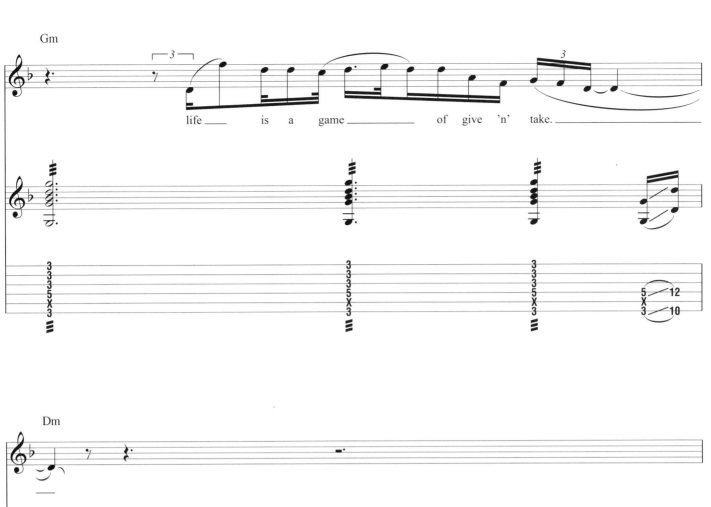

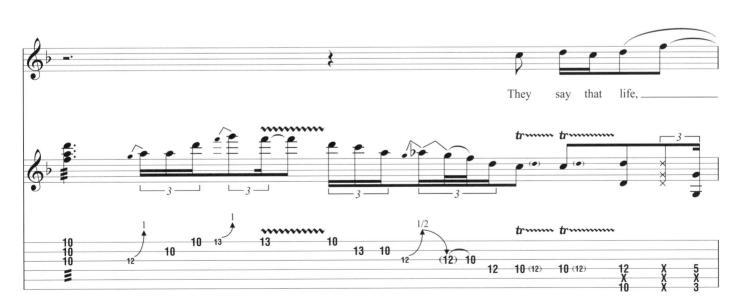

life is a game ___ of give and take. ___

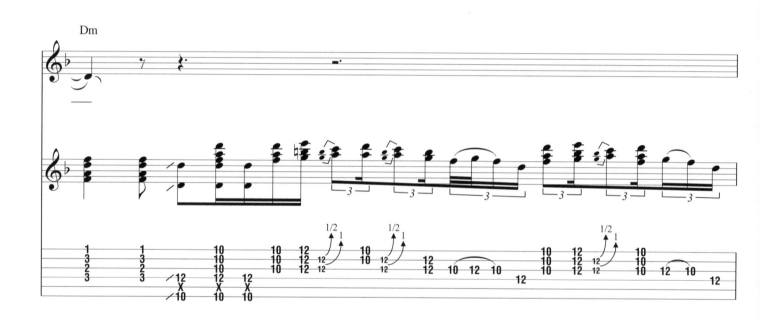

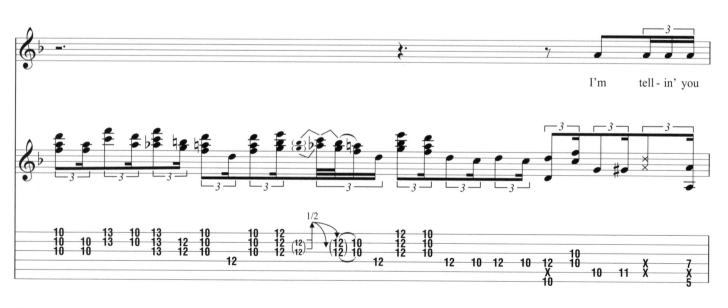

I'm tell - in' you

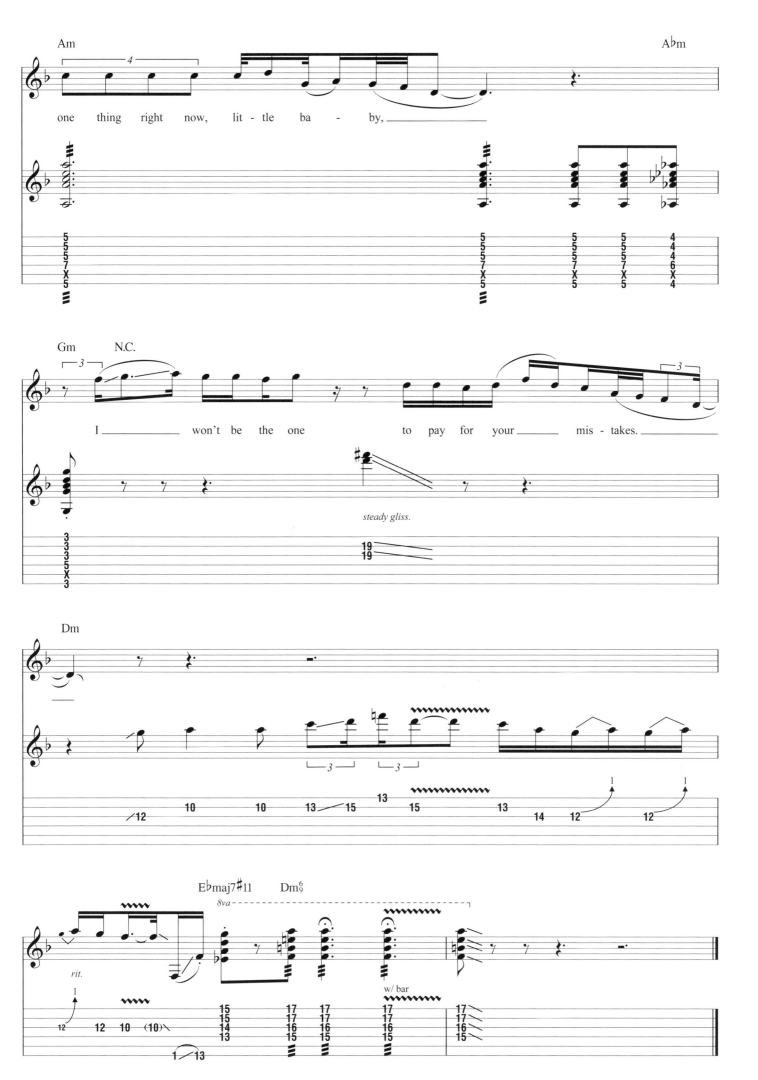

Don't Throw Your Love on Me So Strong

Words and Music by Albert King

Tune down 1 1/2 steps:
(low to high) C#-F#-B-E-G#-C#

Intro

Moderate Blues ♩. = 78

*Symbols in parentheses represent chord names respective to detuned guitar.
Symbols above reflect actual sounding chords.

1. Hey

Verse

ba - by,

you threw your love on me too strong.

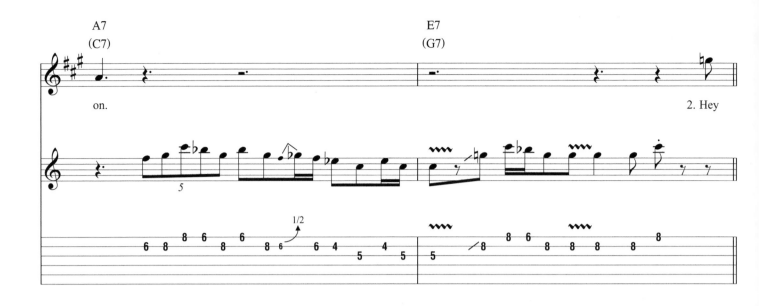

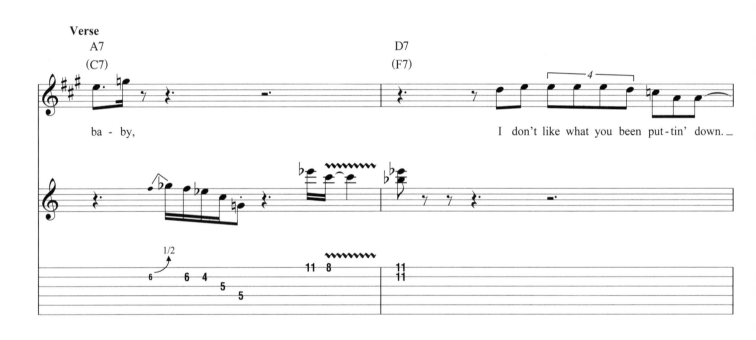

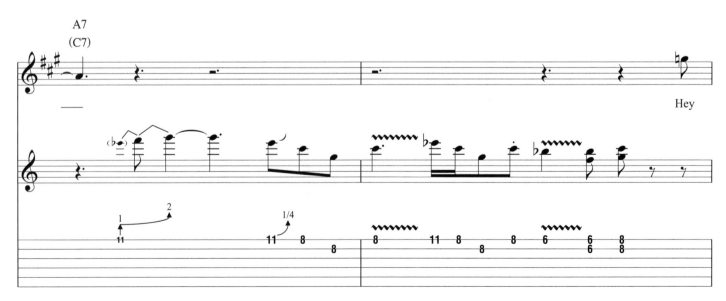

Guitar Solo

A7
(C7)

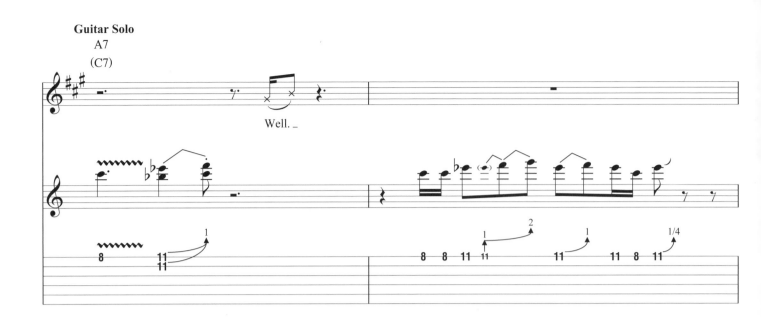

Well.

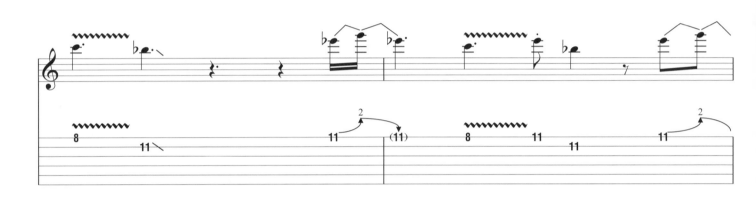

D7
(F7)

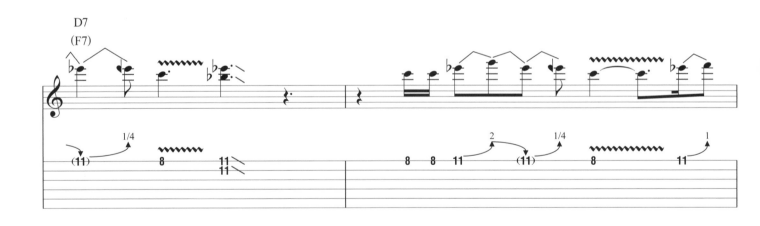

A7
(C7)

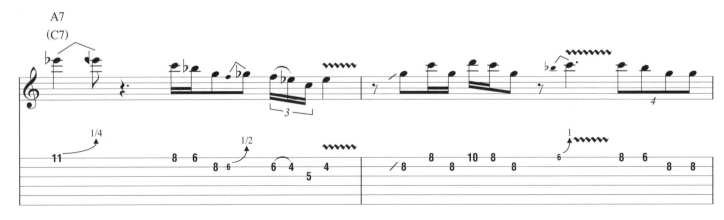

Have You Ever Loved a Woman

Words and Music by Billy Myles

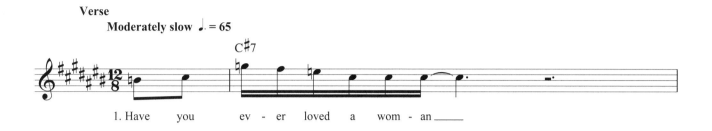

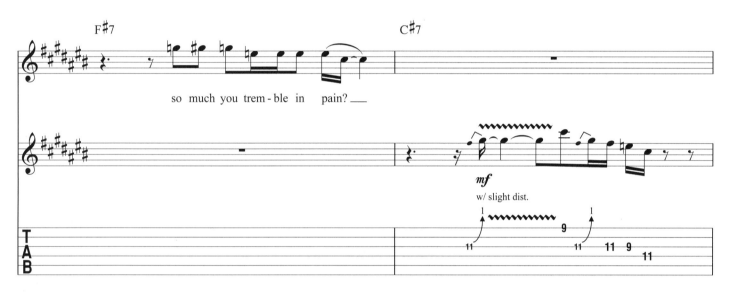

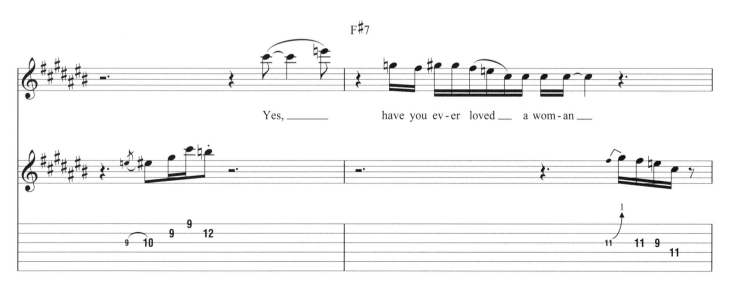

so __ much __ you trem-ble in _____ pain?

Yes, _____ all the time __ you know _____

she __ bears __ an-oth-er man's _____ name. _____

Verse

2. You just love _ that wom-an _

she be - longs __ to your ver - y best _____ friend. _____

Guitar Solo

Five Long Years

Words and Music by Eddie Boyd

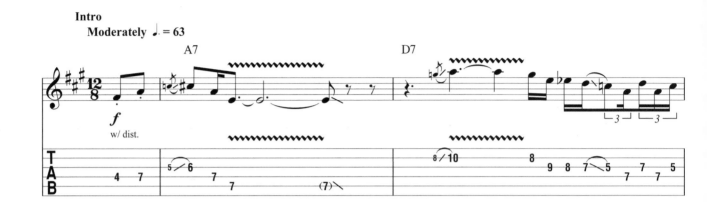

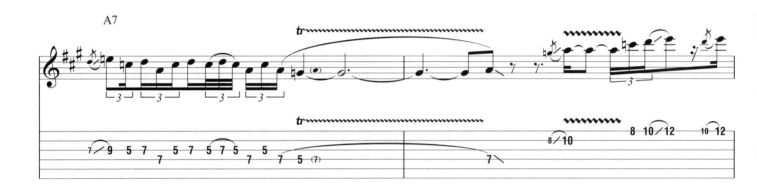

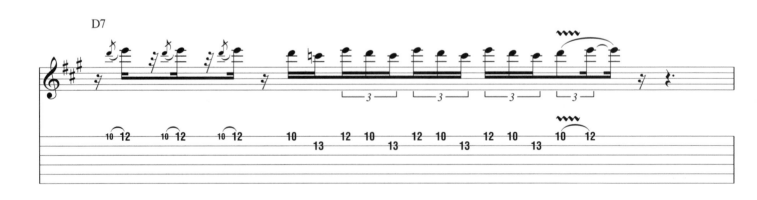

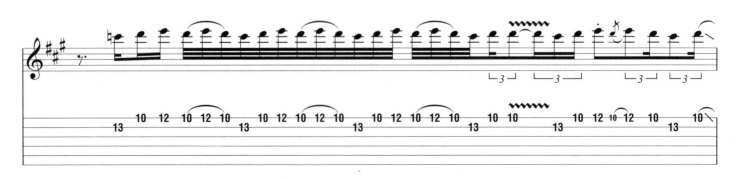

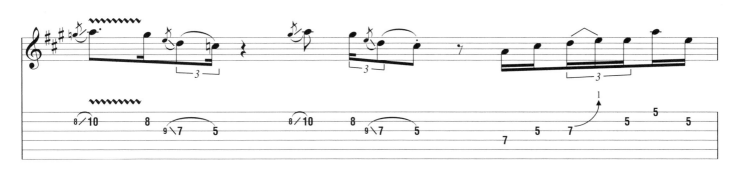

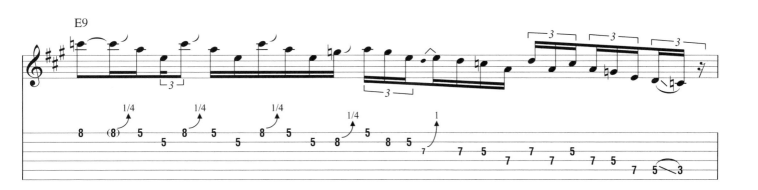

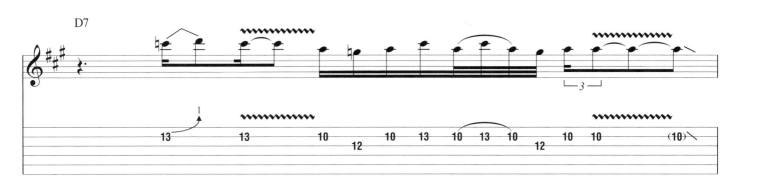

I worked five___ long___ years for___ one wom - an.

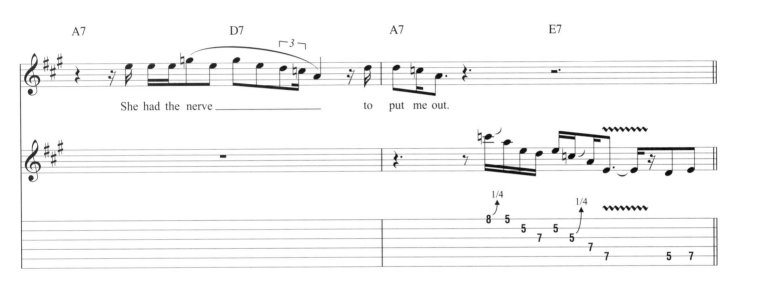

She had the nerve _____ to put me out.

Verse

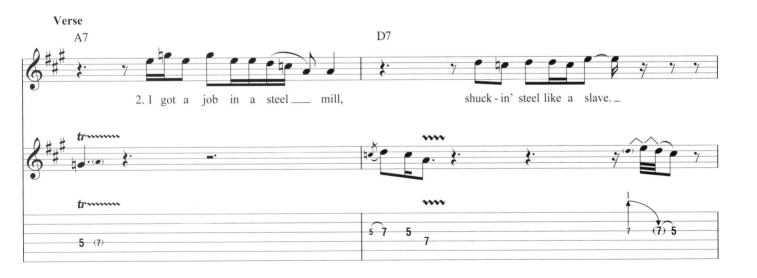

2. I got a job in a steel____ mill, shuck - in' steel like a slave.___

Gtr. tacet

Five___ long___ years ev - 'ry Fri - day I come

straight _ home _ with all _ my pay.

Have you ev-er been mis-

treat - ed?

You know _____ just what I'm talk-

in' a-bout.

I worked five _ long _ years for _ one

wom - an.

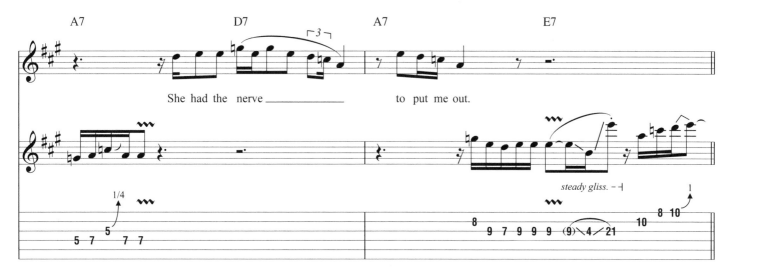

She had the nerve _____ to put me out.

Guitar Solo

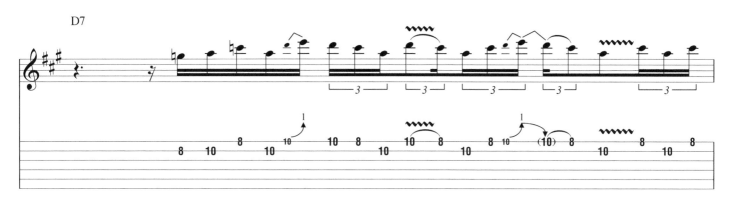

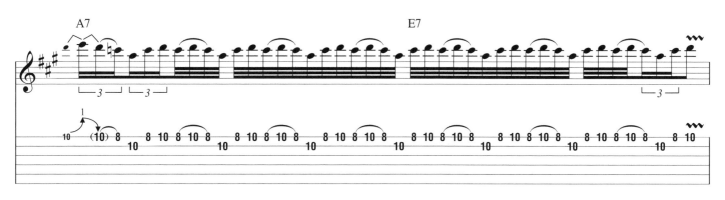

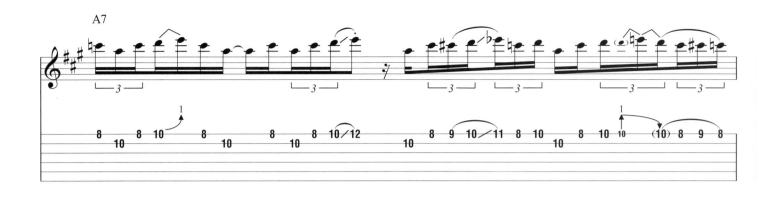

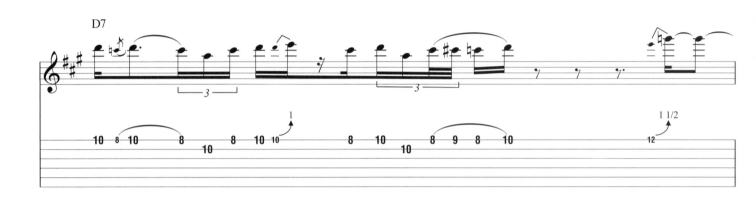

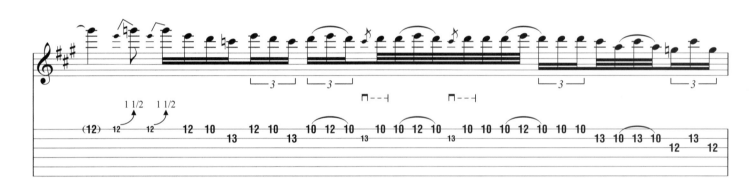

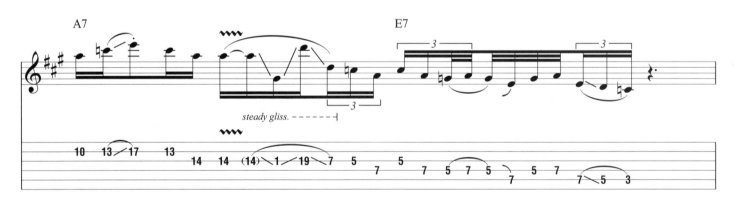

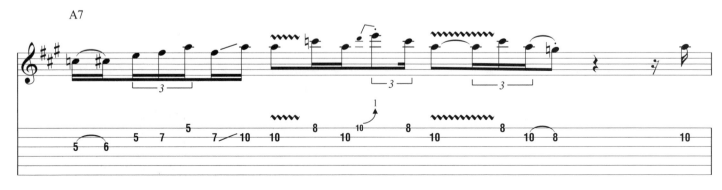

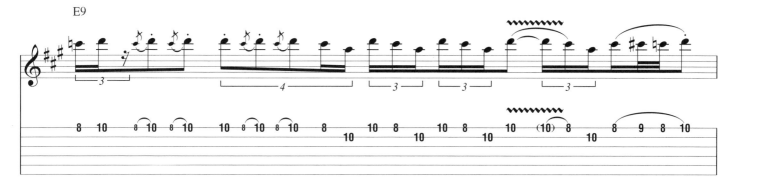

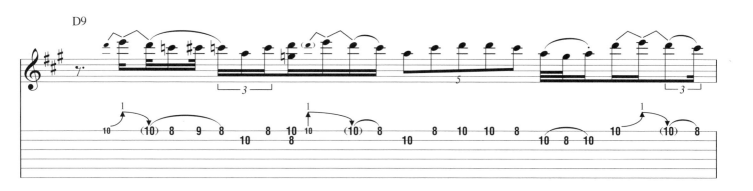

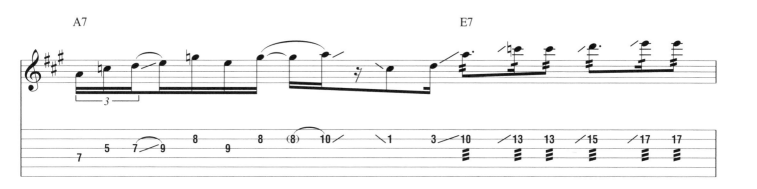

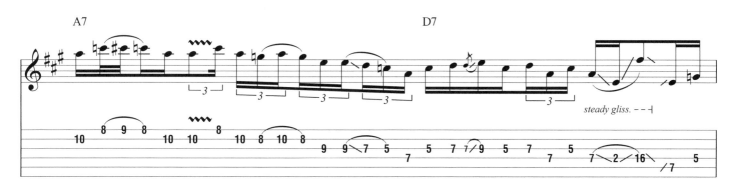

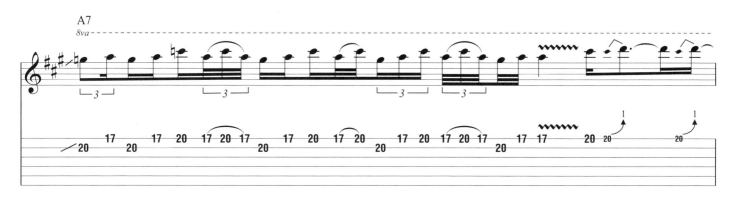

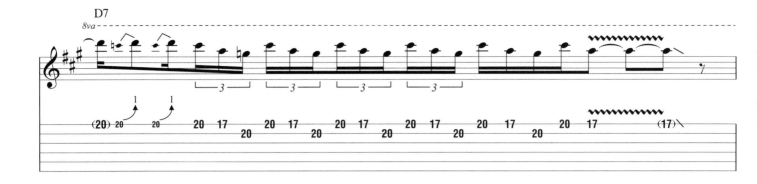

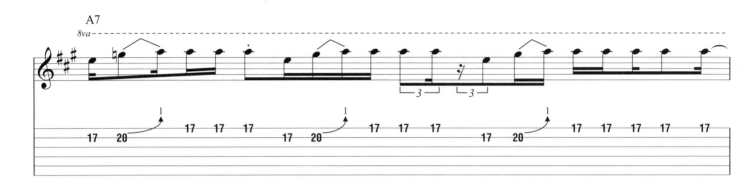

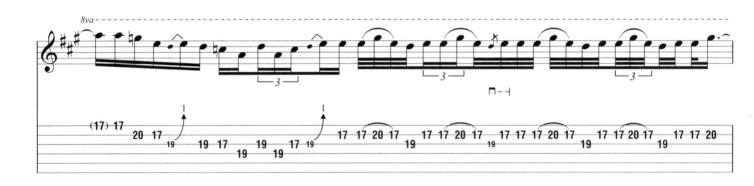

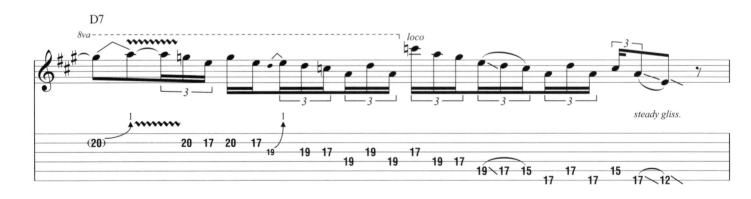

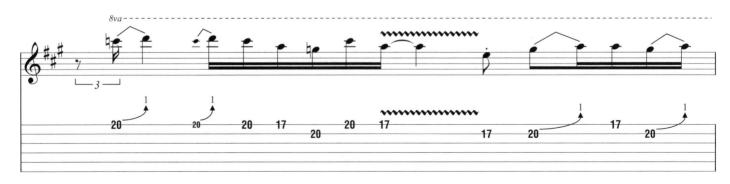

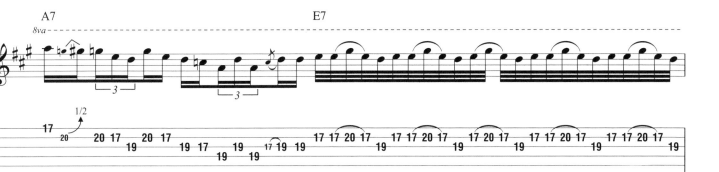

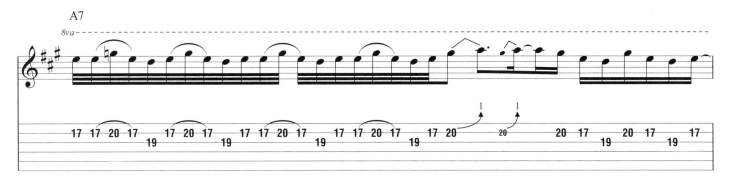

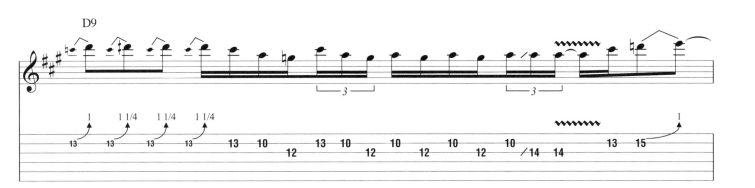

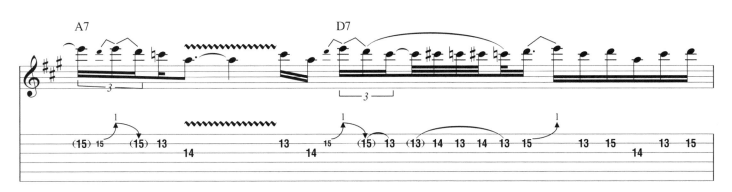

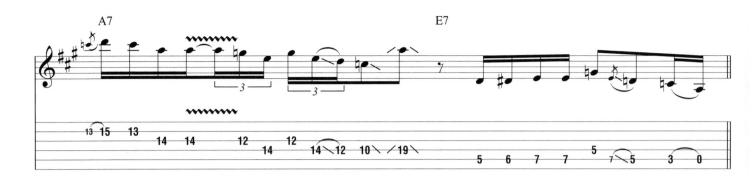

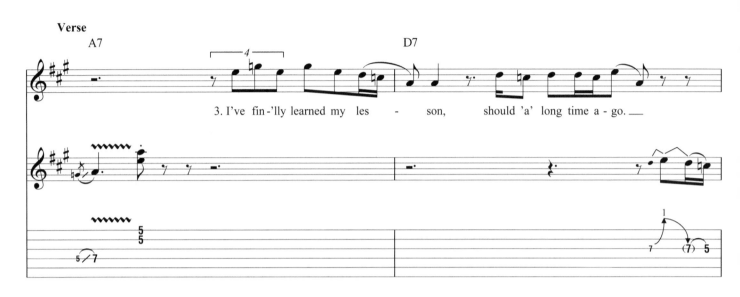

Verse

3. I've fin-'lly learned my les - son, should 'a' long time a - go. ___

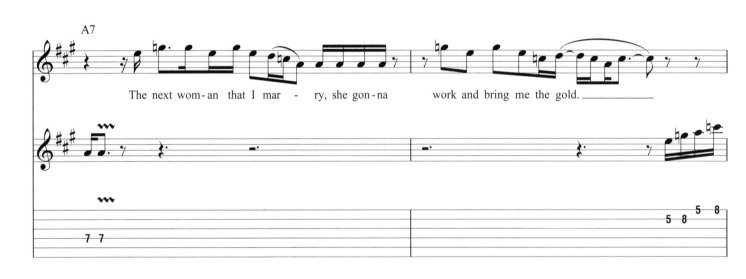

The next wom-an that I mar - ry, she gon-na work and bring me the gold. _____

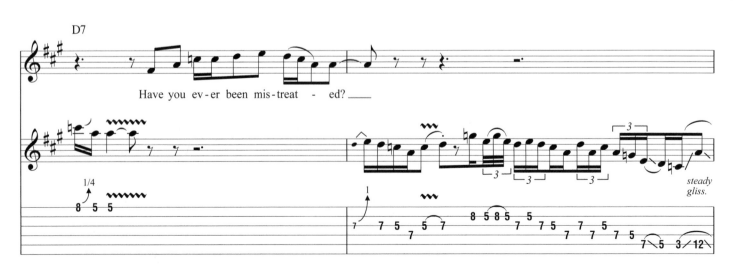

Have you ev-er been mis-treat - ed? ____

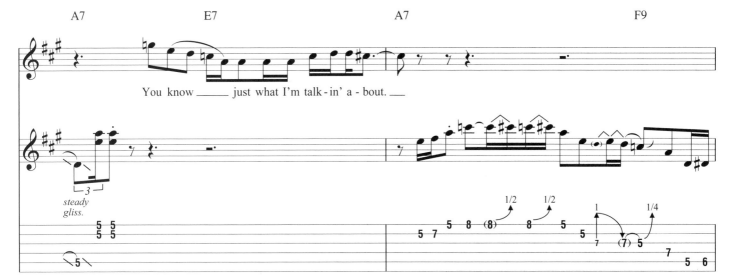

You know _____ just what I'm talk - in' a - bout. _____

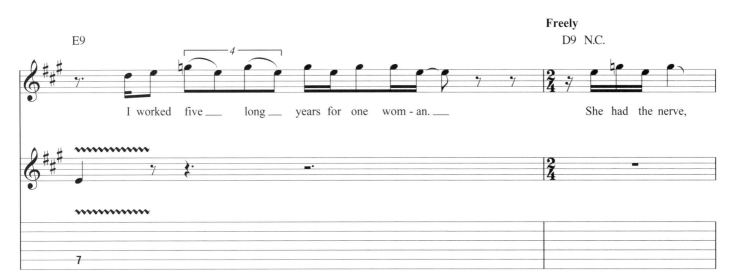

I worked five _____ long _____ years for one wom - an. _____ She had the nerve,

she had the nerve,   she had the nerve,   she had the nerve _____ to put me

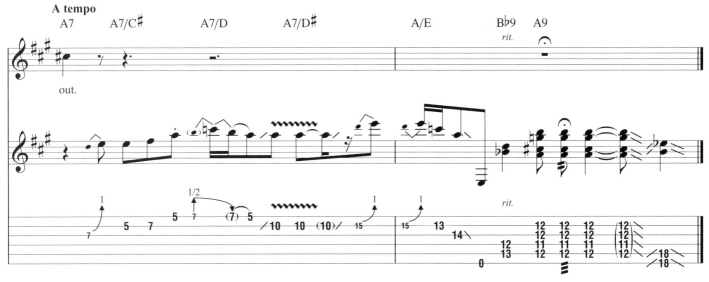

out.

(They Call It) Stormy Monday
(Stormy Monday Blues)
Words and Music by Aaron "T-Bone" Walker

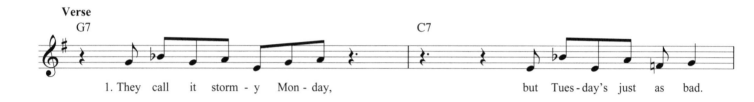

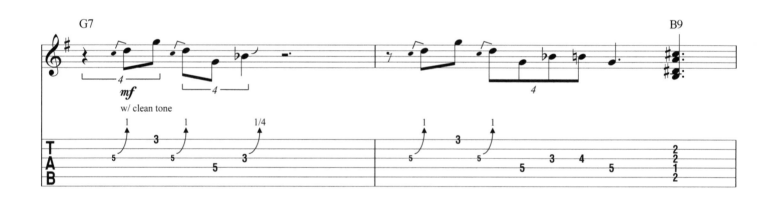

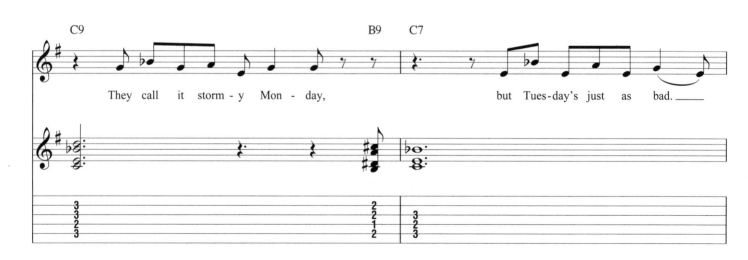

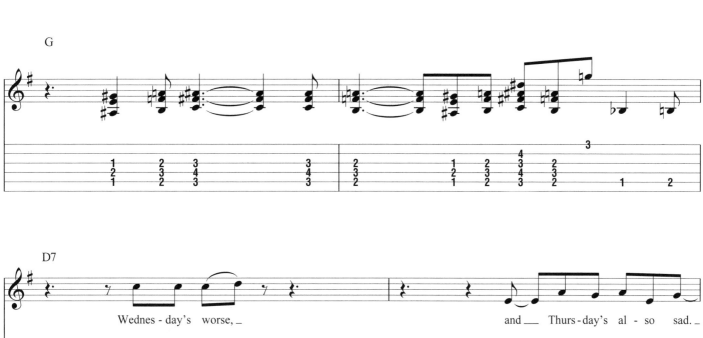

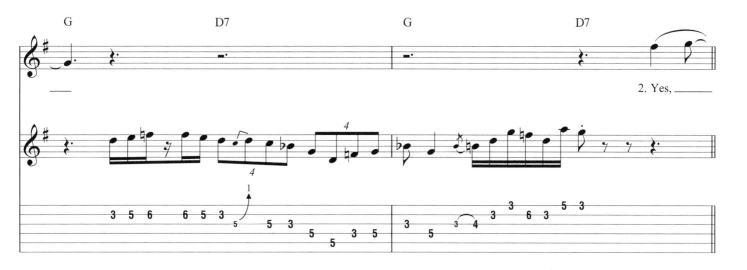

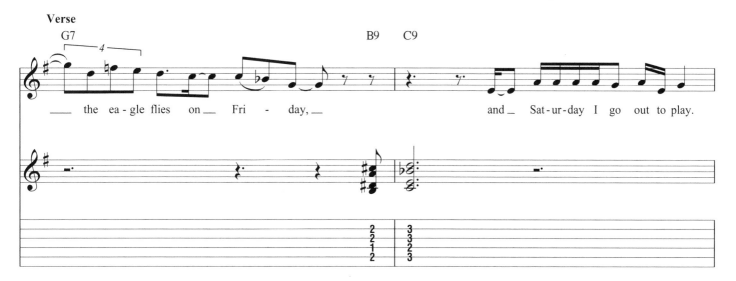

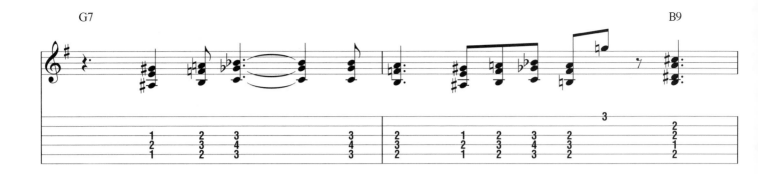

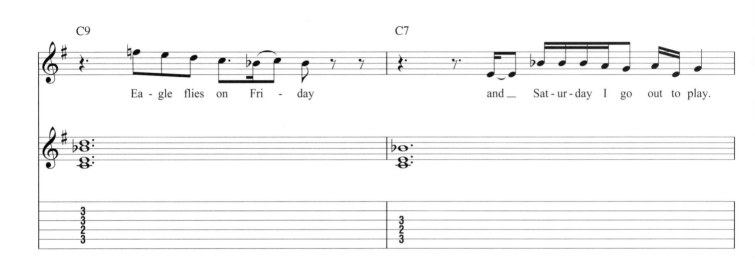

Ea - gle flies on Fri - day   and __ Sat - ur - day I go out to play.

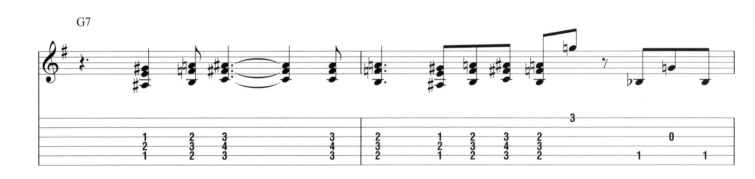

Sun-day I go to church,   then I ____ kneel ____ down and

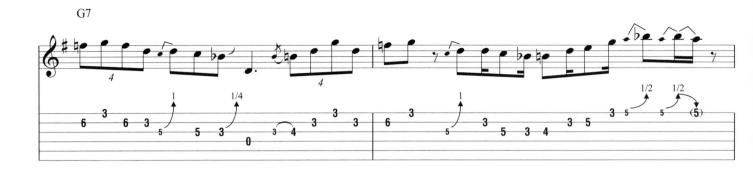

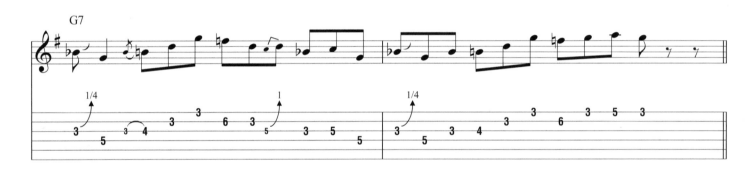

Verse

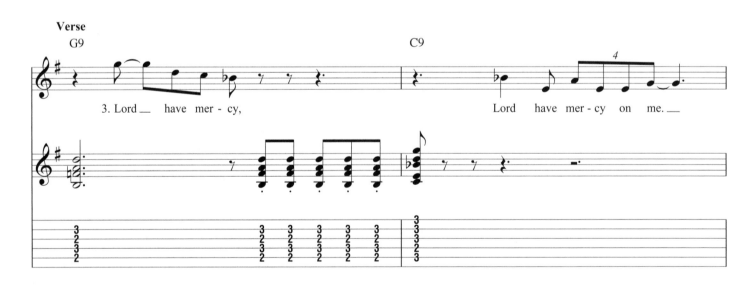

3. Lord ___ have mer - cy,   Lord   have mer - cy   on   me. ___

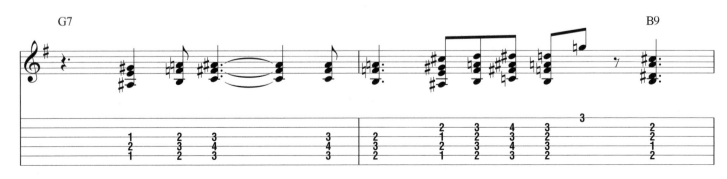

The Things That I Used to Do

Words and Music by Eddie "Guitar Slim" Jones

Capo I

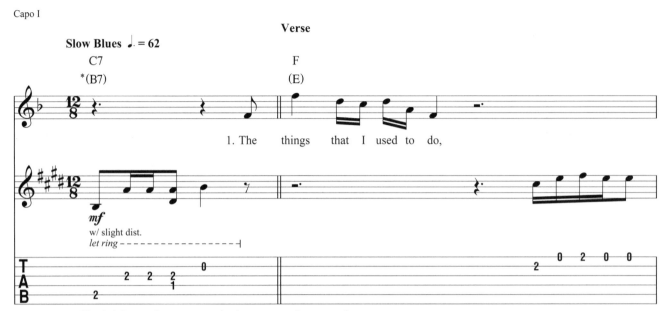

*Symbols in parentheses represent chord names respective to capoed
guitar. Symbols above represent actual sounding chords. Capoed fret is "0" in tab.

that you was hid out   with your oth - er   man.

Guitar Solo

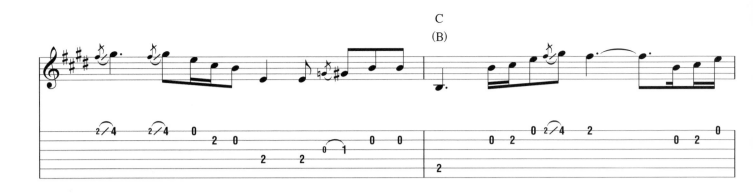

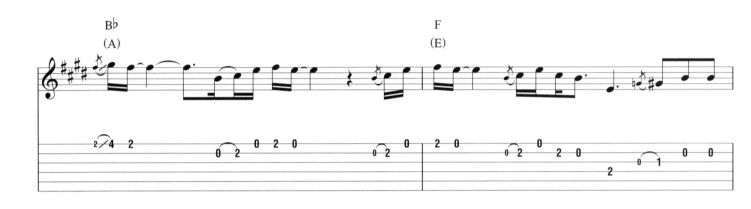

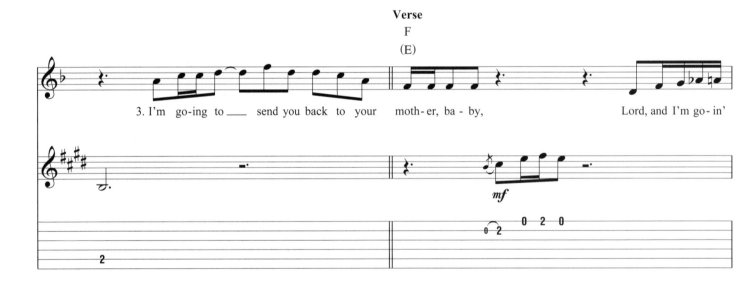

3. I'm go-ing to ___ send you back to your moth-er, ba - by,   Lord, and I'm go-in'

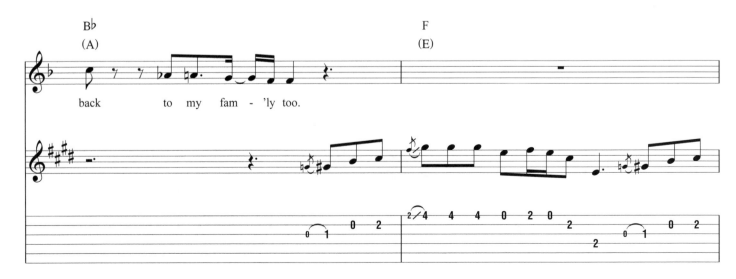

back   to   my   fam - 'ly too.

Three Hours Past Midnight

Words and Music by Johnny Watson and Saul Bihari

Capo III

Intro

Moderately slow ♩. = 65

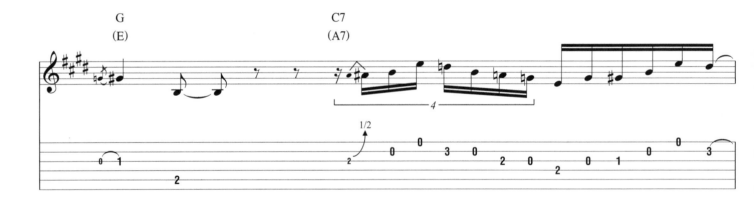

*Symbols in parentheses represent chord names respective to capoed guitar.
Symbols above represent actual sounding chords. Capoed fret is "0" in tab.

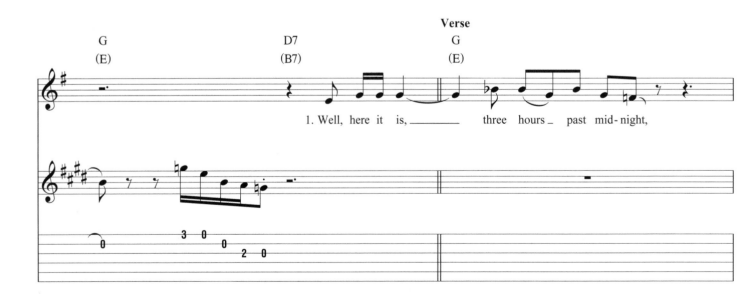

1. Well, here it is, _____ three hours ___ past mid-night,

and I ain't e-ven _____ heard a sound.

2. Yes, _____ I toss and tum-ble on my pil-low,

but I just can't_ close _ my eyes.

Yes, _____ toss and tum-ble on my pil-low,

74

Guitar Solo

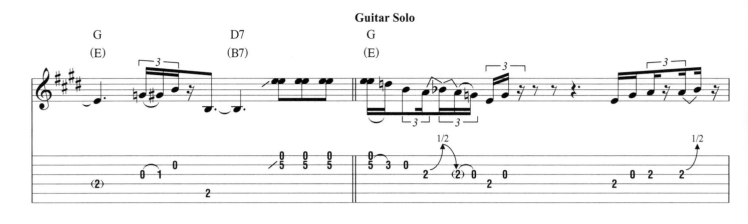

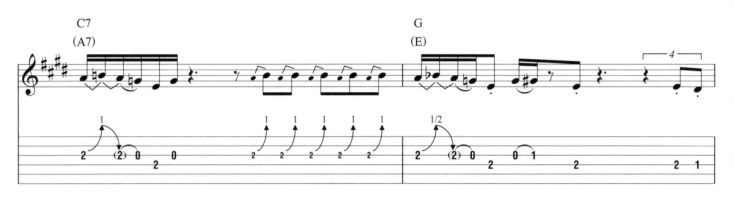

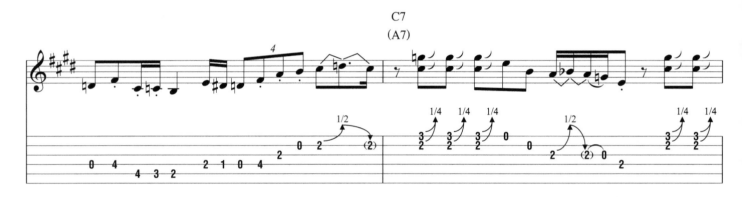

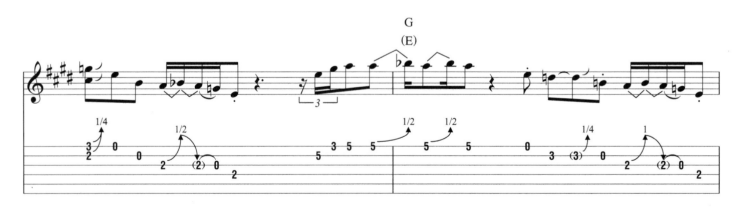

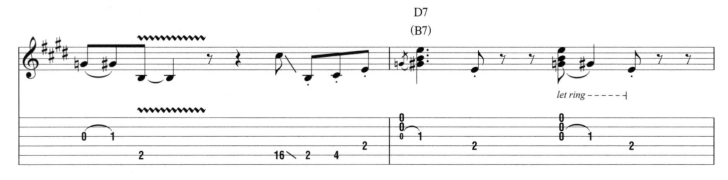

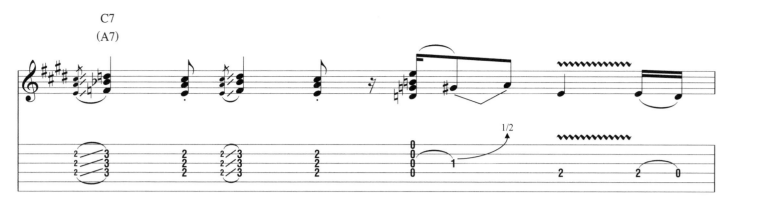

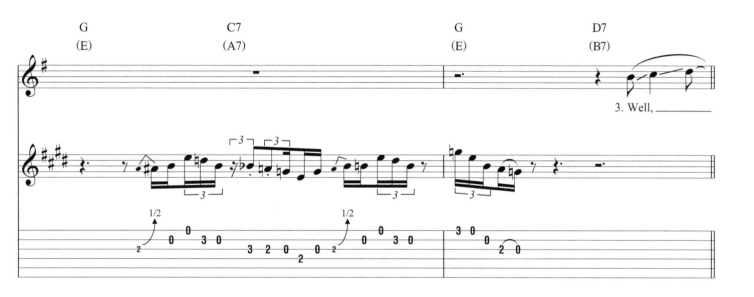

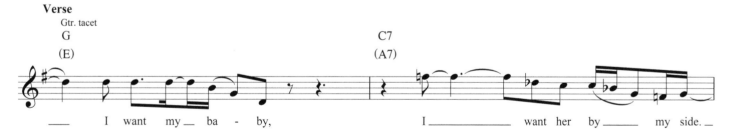

I want my ba - by,   I _____ want her by _____ my side. _____

Well, _____   I

want my ba - by,   yes, I want her by _____ my side. _____

HAL•LEONARD GUITAR PLAY-ALONG®

INCLUDES TAB

is series will help you play your favorite songs quickly and easily. Just follow e tab and listen to the CD to hear how the guitar should sound, and then play ong using the separate backing tracks. Mac or PC users can also slow down e tempo without changing pitch by using the CD in their computer. The melody d lyrics are included in the book so that you can sing or simply follow along.

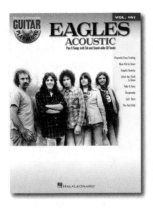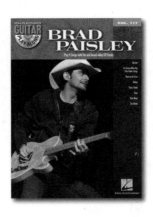

89. REGGAE
00700468 ....$15.99

80. ACOUSTIC ANTHOLOGY
00700175.......................$19.95

81. ROCK ANTHOLOGY
00700176.......................$22.99

82. EASY ROCK SONGS
00700177.......................$12.99

83. THREE CHORD SONGS
00700178.......................$16.99

84. STEELY DAN
00700200.......................$16.99

85. THE POLICE
00700269.......................$16.99

86. BOSTON
00700465.......................$16.99

87. ACOUSTIC WOMEN
00700763.......................$14.99

88. GRUNGE
00700467.......................$16.99

90. CLASSICAL POP
00700469.......................$14.99

91. BLUES INSTRUMENTALS
00700505.......................$14.99

92. EARLY ROCK INSTRUMENTALS
00700506.......................$14.99

93. ROCK INSTRUMENTALS
00700507.......................$16.99

95. BLUES CLASSICS
00700509.......................$14.99

96. THIRD DAY
00700560.......................$14.95

97. ROCK BAND
00700703.......................$14.99

98. ROCK BAND
00700704.......................$14.95

99. ZZ TOP
00700762.......................$16.99

100. B.B. KING
00700466.......................$16.99

101. SONGS FOR BEGINNERS
00701917.......................$14.99

102. CLASSIC PUNK
00700769.......................$14.99

103. SWITCHFOOT
00700773.......................$16.99

104. DUANE ALLMAN
00700846.......................$16.99

106. WEEZER
00700958.......................$14.99

107. CREAM
00701069.......................$16.99

108. THE WHO
00701053.......................$16.99

109. STEVE MILLER
00701054.......................$14.99

111. JOHN MELLENCAMP
00701056.......................$14.99

112. QUEEN
00701052.......................$16.99

113. JIM CROCE
00701058.......................$15.99

114. BON JOVI
00701060.......................$14.99

115. JOHNNY CASH
00701070.......................$16.99

116. THE VENTURES
00701124.......................$14.99

117. BRAD PAISLEY
00701224 ....$16.99

118. ERIC JOHNSON
00701353.......................$16.99

119. AC/DC CLASSICS
00701356.......................$17.99

120. PROGRESSIVE ROCK
00701457.......................$14.99

121. U2
00701508.......................$16.99

123. LENNON & MCCARTNEY ACOUSTIC
00701614.......................$16.99

124. MODERN WORSHIP
00701629.......................$14.99

125. JEFF BECK
00701687.......................$16.99

126. BOB MARLEY
00701701.......................$16.99

127. 1970s ROCK
00701739.......................$14.99

128. 1960s ROCK
00701740.......................$14.99

129. MEGADETH
00701741.......................$16.99

131. 1990s ROCK
00701743.......................$14.99

132. COUNTRY ROCK
00701757.......................$15.99

133. TAYLOR SWIFT
00701894.......................$16.99

134. AVENGED SEVENFOLD
00701906.......................$16.99

136. GUITAR THEMES
00701922.......................$14.99

137. IRISH TUNES
00701966 ....$15.99

138. BLUEGRASS CLASSICS
00701967.......................$14.99

139. GARY MOORE
00702370.......................$16.99

140. MORE STEVIE RAY VAUGHAN
00702396.......................$17.99

141. ACOUSTIC HITS
00702401.......................$16.99

142. KINGS OF LEON
00702418.......................$16.99

144. DJANGO REINHARDT
00702531.......................$16.99

145. DEF LEPPARD
00702532.......................$16.9

147. SIMON & GARFUNKEL
14041591.......................$16.9

148. BOB DYLAN
14041592 ....$16.9

149. AC/DC HITS
14041593.......................$17.9

150. ZAKK WYLDE
02501717.......................$16.9

153. RED HOT CHILI PEPPERS
00702990.......................$19.9

156. SLAYER
00703770 ....$17.9

157. FLEETWOOD MAC
00101382.......................$16.9

158. ULTIMATE CHRISTMAS
00101889.......................$14.9

161. THE EAGLES – ACOUSTIC
00102659.......................$17.9

162. THE EAGLES HITS
00102667.......................$17.9

163. PANTERA
00103036.......................$16.9

166. MODERN BLUES
00700764.......................$16.9

168. KISS
00113421.......................$16.9

169. TAYLOR SWIFT
00115982.......................$16.9

170. THREE DAYS GRACE
00117337.......................$16.9

7777 W. BLUEMOUND RD. P.O. BOX 13819 MILWAUKEE, WI 53213

For complete songlists, visit Hal Leonard online at
www.halleonard.com

Prices, contents, and availability subject to change without notice.